EXTREME SURVIVAL MEAT

A Guide for Safe Scavenging, Pemmican Making, And Roadkill

By Tamarack Song

SNOW WOLF PUBLISHING

Snow Wolf Publishing
7124 Military Road
Three Lakes, Wisconsin 54562
www.snowwolfpublishing.org

Snow Wolf Publishing is a division of Teaching Drum Outdoor School

Song, Tamarack, 1948 –
 Extreme Survival Meat: a guide for safe scavenging, pemmican making, and roadkill / Tamarack Song.

ISBN 978-0-9894737-1-2
1. Sports & Recreation. 2. Outdoor skills.

Text design and layout by Julie Plumitis and Michael Jason Fox.

Illustrations by Melissa Kay Bishop.

To send correspondence to the author of this book, mail a first class letter to the author c/o Snow Wolf Publishing, 7124 Military Road, Three Lakes, Wisconsin 54562, and we will forward the communication, or email the author at info@snowwolfpublishing.org. Visit the author's websites at www.tamaracksong.org, www.teachingdrum.org, and www.brotherwolffoundation.org.

Also by
Tamarack Song

Becoming Nature
Learning the Language of Wild Animals and Plants
to be published Spring 2016

Entering the Mind of the Tracker
Native Practices for Developing Intuitive Consciousness and
Discovering Hidden Nature

Song of the Trusting Heart
A Classic Zen Poem for Daily Meditation

Whispers of the Ancients
Native Tales for Teaching and Healing in Our Time

Journey to the Ancestral Self
The Native Lifeway Guide for Living in Harmony with the Earth
Mother

Tamarack was the major contributor for
Forgiveness and Child Abuse, by Lois Einhorn PhD

CONTENTS

Introduction

3. **Keep Safe.** To protect yourself from communicable diseases, wear protective clothing, glasses, and a bandanna over your nose and mouth, until you have determined the cause of death.

It is important in this assessment process to realize that there is no such thing as a natural death. Every animal dies for a reason, and discovering it will help us determine whether or not the carcass is edible. Oftentimes, the condition of a carcass is not an accurate indicator of the animal's health at the time of death. If the animal laying in front of me has scruffy looking fur, it could be because of disease, or the fur could be falling out due to rot.

None of the following factors in and of themselves will absolutely render an animal inedible other than poisoning and chronic wasting disease. Along with the factors covered here, there are other possibilities, such as hunting and roadkill, which are unlikely to be encountered in long-term survival or wilderness living situations.

Common Causes of Death

If the animal looks well fed and in good shape, with a sleek and shiny pelt, suspect:

- **Poisoning.** If the carcass looks fairly normal, there is no apparent cause of death, and there is drool, vomited blood, and/or black, tarry looking scat, suspect poisoning. Most cases occur in populated areas, and in rural areas around farms and animal operations.
- **Predation.** Signs include torn-up flanks, puncture marks in neck and haunches, and ripped skin. To distinguish predation signs from scavenging signs, the former are generally surface and the latter show torn-out flesh and gut.
- **Accident.** Look for broken bones, puncture wounds, and lacerations. I have seen a bear impaled by a sharp-tipped branch he fell upon, a fawn with legs tangled in branches, and many other odd occurrences.

If the animal looks emaciated or debilitated, with a dull or patchy coat, suspect:

- **Predation.** See above for signs. Predators more often than not kill the old and sick.
- **Parasites.** Though ticks and intestinal worms can theoretically kill an animal, they usually weaken an animal to the point that other factors do her in. Check with regional hunting and trapping organizations and natural resource agencies for parasites that could infect humans.
- **Injury.** An animal may survive an accident, fight, or attack, only to eventually be done in by a resulting infection or debilitating wound.
- **Disease.** Because of the number of wild animal diseases transmissible to humans, many of them being regional, the best sources of relevant information for your area are local health authorities, veterinarians, and game wardens. Following are descriptions of two of the most serious and wide-ranging diseases, along with symptoms to watch for. (In addition, see **Botulism** on pages 13-15.)
    1. **Rabies** is a virus that infects the central nervous system and nearly always causes death. Contracted from the saliva or nerve tissue of an infected animal, the virus can survive for two hours to a week outside the body of a dead animal, and longer inside. The colder the temperature and the more protected from sunlight the virus is, the longer it survives. All it takes to contract rabies is getting a speck of saliva or nerve tissue in your mouth, eyes, or nose, or in a small cut on your hand. Nearly all warm-blooded animals except birds, small rodents, opossums, rabbits, and hares are susceptible and can transmit the disease, usually through biting. Avoid live animals exhibiting any of these symptoms: hyperactivity, aggressiveness, lack of coordination, hind-quarter paralysis, drooling. Wear hand and face protection when handling suspected

animals. Be especially cautious of the common carriers, which in North America are skunks, raccoons, foxes, and bats (in Europe it is the latter two). Thorough cooking kills the virus; boiling is best.

2. **Chronic Wasting Disease (CWD)** is an affliction of the central nervous system caused by a mutated protein called a *prion*. It is found in American elk, moose, and all species of deer. A relatively new and evolving disease, it has rapidly spread to central Canada and all areas of the contiguous US except the far West and Southeast. At present, it is believed to be absent from Alaska and Europe. Closely related to scrapies in sheep, bovine spongiform encephalopathy (BSE) in cattle, and Creutzfeldt-Jakob disease (CJD) in humans, CWD is currently not known to infect humans. However considering its rapidly evolving nature, along with the facts that there is no known cure and all cases are fatal, I strongly encourage complete avoidance of any suspect carcass or live animal. CWD can be contracted by exposure to any part of an infected animal (including urine), the prion can persist for years in the environment, and it cannot be destroyed by cooking. As tempting and easy as they might be to kill, avoid animals showing weight loss, avoidance of other animals, listlessness, lowered head, blank expression, repetitive walking patterns, thin and missing hair, and a faint smell of rotting meat.

CHAPTER 3

Age the Carcass

In and of itself, the time since an animal died is not a determining criteria for edibility. There are many other variables to show whether the animal is edible, which parts are edible—and we will be getting to them shortly. The following indicators can be very helpful when considered along with those in the next step.

- **Blood.** If blood is dripping, is it fresh and bright or dark and crusted over? Is blood in the body cavity fluid or coagulated?
- **Fur.** When you pull on the fur, does it stay tight or pull out? Test different areas of the carcass: the stomach is usually the first place it will slip.
- **Eyes.** Are the eyes bright and full, or cloudy and sunken? How full of fly eggs are they? Are they missing? They are typically the first thing to be scavenged by birds.
- **Rigor Mortis** is the stiffening of the carcass after death. Immediately upon death, the muscles relax and the body flattens out. Rigor mortis then sets in, starting with the head and spreading throughout the body. After a time, it leaves and the carcass again becomes flexible. Warmth speeds up the process, cooling slows it down, and rapid cooling can prevent it. When it starts fast, as is the case with animals wasted away by disease or exhausted by the chase, it passes fast. When the process starts slow, as with healthy, young animals, it passes slowly. Post-rigor mortis meat, which is more tender than fresh, is favored by many.

- **Fly Eggs/Maggots.** Eggs can appear almost immediately on a carcass, in orifices and wounds. How many are there? Maggots soon follow; are they small or large, and how numerous are they? How much of the animal have they consumed?

- **Bloating** is caused by methane gas from the normal fermentation of stomach contents. With ungulates (hooved animals), fermentation continues after death; however the gas does not escape, so bloating occurs. Has it progressed to the point where it is inflating areas beyond the gut and separating skin from flesh? In extreme cases, nearly the entire animal can be ballooned out. Accompanied by increasing discoloration of the gut area (see *Stomach Greening* on page 11).

- **Scavenger Sign.** The older a carcass, the more likely it is to be scavenged, and the more will be missing. Note how fresh or crusted over their incursions are. Scavenger openings provide a good place for assessing the condition of the flesh and inner organs.

- **Precipitation.** If it has rained or snowed recently, is it dry under the carcass, or is there snow/dampness? That will tell you whether the animal was killed before or after precipitation.

- **Temperature** either speeds up or slows down every indicator but *Scavenger Sign* and *Precipitation*, and this fact makes it virtually impossible to attach specific times to aging indicators. In hot weather, a carcass can become a stinking mass of maggots in just a couple of days; whereas in below-freezing temperatures, it can remain fresh for months. Let common sense and experience be your guides.

Carcass-Aging Exercise

Use the chart below to learn carcass aging by noting your daily observations as carcasses degrade over time in various environmental conditions. You can speed up the learning process by charting more than one carcass at a time.

Species:	Date:		Cause of Death:		
	Day 1	Day 2	Day 3	Day 4	Etc.
Ave. Air Temp					
Ground Temp					
% Sun					
Precipitation					
Blood					
% Fur Slippage					
Eyes					
Rigor Progression					
Fly Eggs/Maggots					
Bloating					
Scavenger Sign					
% Left					

CHAPTER 4

Assess Condition and Edibility

An animal can smell and look terrible, yet believe it or not, have edible body parts. Most animals, especially herbivores, start rotting in the belly, and from there it gradually spreads to the extremities. The belly could be a pool of seething maggots, yet portions of the thigh, shoulder, and shank muscles could still be edible, along with the bone marrow. The following indicators give the information needed to make safe and intelligent decisions.

External Signs
- **Stomach Greening.** Look for bluish-green to purple coloration in the gut area. The deeper and more extensive the discolored area, the less likely internal organs are edible. Yet the rest of the animal could still be safe to eat. If the meat has an off taste from the stomach content fermentation gases, eat it in moderation.
- **Smell.** Generally speaking, the smellier the animal, the less likely it is to be edible, or the less of the animal will be edible. Our sense of smell is a trusty guide, as we are biologically wired to gag at rotten meat. As part of the carcass-aging exercise above, practice learning to distinguish between the smell of stomach gas and the smell of rotting meat.
- **Maggots.** Even though it is commonly believed that if there are maggots, the carcass is no longer edible, the presence of

maggots has nothing to do with edibility. Ignore them and go on with your assessment but do not ignore them completely, as they are edible.

- **Fleas.** The presence of fleas means that the animal has recently died and could be entirely edible, as fleas will abandon an animal as soon as there is no more fresh blood to suck.
- **Ripped-Open Gut.** Most predators and scavengers will go for the gut first, which is good for those of us coming second. With the putrefying gut removed, the carcass could remain edible for days longer.
- **Killer/Scavenger Contamination.** Some animals will mark their kills with scat or urine, and their saliva can transmit communicable diseases (refer back to *Common Causes of Death* on pages 5 and 6).
- **Variable Rotting.** One part of an animal may be exposed to hot air or sunlight, thereby degrading quickly, while another area may be preserved by being in contact with the cold ground or ice.

> **Haste Makes Waste**
> Never forgo a carcass on first impression. *In a survival situation, you cannot afford to.* Go through every external and internal assessment listed here, in hope of finding even the smallest portion that might be edible. It could make the difference between life and death.

Internal Signs
- **Mouth.** With a non-ruminant, and when the gut is intact, the mouth can be an important first indicator of edibility. If the mouth is open, is the tongue pale, dry, and shriveled, or is it moist and succulent looking? Assess any juice draining from the mouth (push on the gut to encourage more): does it smell acrid and sour, or of bile and rot?

- **Organs.** Assess the color and texture of the heart, liver, kidneys, and lungs. Cut each organ in half to check the interior condition. Organs are generally the first part of the animal to rot, so if they are good, the rest of the animal is likely to be also. Learn what healthy organs should look and feel like by helping with butchering (see the next chapter).
- **Liver.** This is the indicator organ, as it breaks down quickly and often shows signs of disease, so we need to give it special attention. Does it have its typical deep, rich color and resilient, spongy texture? When you slice into it, does the cut retain its sharp edge? If it shows any off-colored blotches, mushy areas, or odd shape, discard the entire carcass, sanitize your hands, and either sanitize or dispose of your outer clothing.
- **Smell.** Check the odor of all surfaces of a questionable organ or chunk of meat. Keep taking slices off of rotten-smelling area until you detect no more odor.
- **Exploded Guts.** Fecal matter and bile can be washed from the meat and organs of an animal with a freshly exploded gut, with no ill effect to the meat and little or no effect on its flavor. Even when the meat has been marinated in bile and fecal matter, it is still edible in moderation, as long as the meat meets all other criteria for being edible.
- **Color of Meat.** The muscle tissue of mammals is typically a deep red, and it turns brown as it ages, starting on the surface. If it is brown, slice through its center to see if the interior might yet be red. Trim the brown from the red and process it separately. Eat brown meat only as a last resort, even if it checks out in all other ways.

Shouldn't it Be Okay if Other Animals are Eating It?

If we had their iron stomachs and immune systems, the answer would be "yes." Unfortunately, there are the little matters of **Botulism** and **Trichinosis**. *Clostridium botulinum*, a bacterium related to anthrax, cholera, and salmonella causes Botulism. The botulinum organism itself is harmless; however, it produces an odorless, tasteless nerve suppressant, which is *the most potent toxin known*. It takes so little of the toxin to constitute a lethal dose that you cannot afford to even think about tasting suspect meat.

The first symptom, which appears from 8 to 36 hours after ingestion, is facial paralysis in the form of droopy eyelids and trouble seeing and talking. Then it spreads throughout the body, interfering with breathing and eventually causing respiratory failure. Without medical treatment, you stand only a one-in-three chance of surviving.

Many mammals, amphibians, birds, and even some invertebrates, are susceptible to botulism infections. The dog, cat, and swine families are resistant. Waterfowl, on the other hand, are very prone to the disease, so hold suspect any dead or dying that you come across. If you were fortunate enough to have seen the animal before she died and noticed that she was drooling or agitated, along with showing progressive paralysis, expect botulism.

Animals typically become infected either by eating botulinium-infected animals, or by foraging in the anaerobic (oxygen-free) environments that bacteria need to sustain themselves. The high incidence of botulism in waterfowl is due to the anaerobic conditions of shallow ponds. It turns out that carcasses also provide a favorable anaerobic environment.

A number of carrion scavengers, such as vultures, coyotes, and hyenas, have naturally-occurring botulism toxin antibodies, along with very strong immune systems. Vultures can handle 900 times the toxin load we can. With a pH near zero, their guts are nearly 10 times more acidic than those of eagles, hawks, and other carnivorous birds. We, on the other hand, are on the very low end of the toxin-tolerance spectrum.

So what are we supposed to do when our group is facing starvation and we are staring down at an elk carcass that could feed us for days, yet it might be botulism infected? There is a way, but only if we follow these instructions precisely.

To Safely Eat Botulism-Infected Meat

1. **Do not eat raw.** This includes every part of the animal. Do not even taste.

2. **Render the toxin inactive** by either heat or ultraviolet radiation. Here are three effective wilderness methods:
   - **Boil for 10 minutes.** Dice or slice small to assure that the interior reaches boiling temperature for the entire time.
   - **Roast over fire.** Slice ultrathin and hold close to flame or coals until crisp and completely dry.
   - **Expose to sunlight.** Slice ultrathin and lay out with full exposure to the midday sun, for three hours on each side, making a total of six hours. The slices do not have to be completely dried.

3. **Take no risks.** There is virtually nothing that can be done for you if you end up with botulism—the worst form of food poisoning.

Do not worry about trying to kill the botulism organisms themselves, as it is highly unlikely that they will infect healthy adults. How fortunate we are that the organisms are harmless to most, as they are resistant to drying and ultraviolet light, and they can survive boiling for up to four hours. Killing them in food requires bringing the internal temperature to 250° for 30 minutes, which is virtually impossible to achieve without a pressure cooker.

Trichinosis, the other raw-meat scourge to watch out for, is a parasitic infection caused by microscopic roundworms of the Trichinella genus. The infection is spread by ingesting worm cysts in uncooked meat and fat. Common carriers are bear, swine, bobcat, wolf, coyote, fox, walrus, seal, raccoon, skunk and other small omnivores and carnivores. Horses can be carriers, although cases are very rare.

The first symptoms to show in humans are abdominal discomfort, nausea, diarrhea fatigue, and fever. They can be followed by muscle pain, aching joints, facial swelling, fever and chills, headaches, and constipation. Abdominal symptoms may appear as soon as one or two days after ingestion, and symptoms can persist for up to three months before the infection clears. A heavy infection can result in death.

Drying will not kill all of the cysts, and neither will smoking, salting, or freezing. However, the good news is that the cysts are easily destroyed by thorough cooking. If we were preparing the fresh meat for immediate consumption, all we would have to do is bring its core temperature up to 160°F for a few minutes.

Of course in a survival situation very few of us will have meat thermometers in our back pockets, so here is what to do:

To Kill Trichinella Cysts

1. **Roast or boil** the meat until you think it is heated clear through.
2. **Slice open** at its thickest part. If the center is just about to start steaming, or if you can't keep your finger inserted in the meat for more than a second or two, you have reached 160°.
3. **Return to heat** for a few extra minutes, just to be sure.

How to Safely Chew the Fat

Fat is more valuable for its life-giving energy than any other food. It packs over twice the calories of starch, sugar, or protein, and it gives sustaining energy, as opposed to sugar's buzz-and-crash. Without fat, long-term wilderness survival is near-impossible. We want to go all out in salvaging every speck of fat we can from a carcass.

The two commonly known body fats are *subcutaneous*, which is found under the skin, and *organ* (or *visceral*), which cushions and protects the internal organs. While subcutaneous fat is the softer of the two and cooks and renders the most easily, it also spoils the quickest, so eat it first. Organ fat can become quickly contaminated from the gut contents, so remove it immediately and either eat it or store it according to the guidelines below.

Most animals go through seasonal cycles where they build up fat reserves for the coming lean season, for winter, or for hibernation. This is followed by a lean period where they begin the cycle anew. If our carcass is shy on visible fat, here are some little-known reserves we cannot afford to miss.

The Invisible Fat
- **Brain.** Has 60% fat content. Eat whole or render (see rendering instructions in chapter 7).
- **Spinal column.** Like the brain, it contains fat. Separate vertebrae to extract.
- **Bones.** Crack open the large, round bones to extract the marrow, which is 80% fat.
- **Feet of ungulates.** Remove hooves and boil with shinbone, skimming the rendered oil off the top.
- **Bird skins.** Fat content varies with species and time of year. Boil and skim the rendered oil off the top.

Now that we have the fat, we need to determine its edibility. Most animal fats are unstable in their raw state. When an animal dies, her body fat starts to go rancid, which is a breakdown process caused by either exposure to oxygen or microbial activity. In either case, byproducts are produced that render the fat inedible. Offensive smell and taste are just the beginning. By eating rancid fat, we could end up with protein, fat, and vitamin deficiencies, along with a range of health issues, including cancer. The risk pertains not just to fat per se, but to bones, skin, meat, and any other tissues that contain fat.

Practice is the best teacher when it comes to assessing fat and fatty foods. Prepare yourself for a survival situation by taking opportunities to help hunters and trappers process their game. Processing roadkill, which is covered in the next chapter, offers another option for training. Here is a guide you can use while processing, as well as when your survival is at stake.

Fat Edibility Assessment

- **Smell.** Fresh fat has a pleasant odor that is sometimes reminiscent of the animal. You might detect the light scent of flesh or blood. If it smells sharp or pungent, suspect rancidity. The warmer the fat, the stronger the odor; so to test it, warm a sample. Another method is to concentrate the essence by enclosing the fat in a container.
- **Taste.** Fresh fat is mild tasting, with subtle flavors unique to each animal. When fat goes rancid, it takes on overtones that people variously describe as bitter, cardboardy, sour, metallic, pungent, or acrid. Whatever the description, they have two qualities in common: they linger, and to varying degrees, they burn the back of the throat.
- **Color.** Ranging from solid colored to translucent, fresh fat can be creamy white, dull yellow, light brown, or anything in between. When it goes rancid, it becomes dirty looking, taking on a shade of beige or gray.
- **Texture.** In some animals, fresh fat will feel firm, and in others, it will have a gel-like quality. When it goes rancid, it gets mushy and the surface can become scummy or slimy.

Our bodies can handle a small amount of rancidity. In fact, the flavor of some of our favorite foods, such as aged cheeses and processed meats, are the result of rancidification. However, rancid food should not constitute a normal part of our diet, whether at home or in the wilderness, for reasons previously mentioned. If it is strongly rancid, *do not eat it*, even if you are desperate. You could quickly end up incapacitated by severe abdominal cramping, nausea, and diarrhea.

Yet there are uses for rancid fat. Set it aside to employ as a lubricant, leather treatment, waterproofer, and for making fat lamps/candles.

One Last Chance

Before we toss that fat onto the utility pile, let's give it one final test. Some fat, especially thick chunks, can insulate themselves from spoilage, sometimes for a surprising amount of time. I once came across a piece of fat in a plastic bag that I had set aside in the garage three years prior, and the interior was still edible. It was one of those fats that have the ability to restrict spoilage to just its surface area.

To Assess Old Fat

1. **Cut through the thickest section**, so that you can view a cross-section.
2. **Compare the exterior with the Interior**, using the *Fat Edibility Assessment*. If the interior tests out as edible,
3. **Trim off the surface rot**, cook, and eat.

CHAPTER 5

Practice on Roadkill

Nearly all of what we have covered thus far can be practiced on roadkill. Think of a vehicle as a predator. Old age, disease, and injury, along with youth and mating behavior, can put animals at high risk of both vehicle collisions and predation. Whether in urban areas, the suburbs, or the countryside, birds, reptiles, and mammals are continually being hit. Whether or not you elect to incorporate roadkill into your diet, you can certainly use them to hone your survival skills.

However, before we get into that, I would like to put in a plug for eating roadkill, as it can reduce our food budgets and nourish us with the very best quality protein. Despite the jokes and stigma that surround eating roadkill, some see it as making the best of the needless deaths caused by vehicles. Oftentimes, the only difference between roadkill and hunted meat is the way in which the animal was killed. When we pick up an animal from alongside the road, it offers us the opportunity to eat wild, organic meat as well as hone our survival skills.

Where I live, vehicle-killed deer and other animals are a normal part of the roadside scenery. Countless people pass them by, allowing their precious flesh to either rot beside the road or feed other scavengers. I regularly bring home deer carcasses, along with turtles, pheasants, turkeys, squirrels, rabbits, and others, and I have been doing so for fifty years. And I am not alone: in some regions, roadkill scavenging is a commonly accepted practice. With a little cleaning and dressing, my family and I regularly eat free-range, organic meat for free, with plenty to share when guests drop by.

When roadkill is gathered and processed intelligently, following the three steps covered in the previous chapter, then the health risks are very low. After eating thousands of roadkill meals, I have never gotten sick; whereas I have had a couple of cases of food poisoning from store-bought meat.

There is also the survival aspect of roadkill to consider. This book is primarily a guide for long-term wilderness survival situations, as well as for those who choose to live by their wits in the wilds. At the same time, there are people whose everyday lives are matters of survival. I've known homeless people, struggling families, and hermits, whose situations would be all the more desperate if it were not for the regular meals the highway provided.

Whatever our philosophy, and whatever our motivation, the bottom line is that in a life or death situation, we can only eat what is available. The time to learn that skill is now, when we have the luxury to do so. If we wait until it slaps us in the face, not only are we going to suffer, but so will those who have come to rely on us. I encourage you to consider roadside carrion a gift, and to have fun learning to use it with your family and friends.

Legalities

Regulations vary widely regarding roadkill utilization, from rural areas in the US where people do largely what they please, to places like Germany, where it is illegal to pick up or utilize any kind of roadkill. In most areas of the US, species that are governed by either hunting or trapping regulations will have salvage restrictions. Federal regulations prohibit the possession of migratory birds and raptors, and any parts thereof. And then there are strict protected, threatened, and endangered species regulations.

This may sound overwhelming and prohibitive, however, salvage permits or tags are often available for some common species. Throughout most of the US, there are unregulated species with abundant populations, and roadkills are free for the grabbing. When there are regulations, the level of enforcement varies from region to region.

How to Inform Yourself

First: familiarize yourself with regulations on the local, state, and federal level that could potentially affect you, so that you are well informed of the legal parameters.

Second: contact your local game warden, forest ranger, or other wildlife official, to see which regulations they enforce, and how to secure necessary permits.

Third: talk with locals. Hunters, trappers, and foragers you have trusting relationships with can fill you in on what roadkill salvagers and officials actually do in practice.

Salvaging Guidelines

- **Gather early in the day**, especially in summertime. Many animals are hit at night, and they will degrade if they lay all day in the hot sun.
- **Stay informed of disease outbreaks** in your area, along with the species that are affected.
- **Bypass chronic disease vectors** such as Norway Rats. Check with your local health authorities for other species to avoid.
- **Avoid pets,** both out of consideration for their owners, and because their diets and lifestyles render them unwholesome. As a kindness, report tagged animals to their owners.
- **Be cautious of animals in populated and agricultural areas**, where poisoning, parasite, and disease rates can be high. The more populated the area, the more garbage scavengers eat. Rabbits, squirrels, most birds, and muskrats in unpolluted wetlands, have relatively clean diets.
- **Be discreet.** Even though what you are doing may be within the limits of the law, consider being careful with

what you tell people, along with keeping a low profile. There are people—even some officials—who have biases regarding the consumption of roadkill, and there could be people with prejudices and suspicions who could cause you trouble.

Processing and Preserving

Most of us will have a variety of available options for gaining roadkill processing skills. Experience is the best teacher, and there are usually people around who are glad to pass along their know-how. Here are some suggestions to get you started.

Where to Learn Processing Skills

- **Fellow foragers and survival trainees.** They are often the best bet, as they have shared values and lifestyle.
- **Hunters and trappers.** Some of them are dedicated to passing their skills on to the next generation, and sometimes a person just plain appreciates the help.
- **Wild game processors.** Small operators in particular might appreciate the extra help in exchange for training.
- **Game wardens.** Typically knowing a good share of the outdoor-oriented people in the area, they can give you referrals.
- **Hunting clubs.** Most are socially oriented organizations, with members willing to help.
- **Outdoor skills schools.** Some teach trapping, skinning, tanning, and processing.
- **Books and online guides.** Your local library and the internet can provide you with a wealth of information.

Processing Tips for Roadkill and Carrion

1. **Gut the animal immediately** and hang in a cool, shaded area, to get the carcass chilled down and forestall rot. Right away separate organs from guts.

Be Careful Slitting Open the Belly
Too deep a cut might puncture the stomach or gut, which could contaminate the organs—especially with a bloated animal.

2. **Determine edibility** with the method given in Chapter 4.
3. **Process as soon as possible.**
   - Separate spoiled meat from good meat.
   - Be very careful not to puncture scent glands or contaminate flesh with excrement. Here is a statement from one of my students: "It was my first roadkill, a porcupine, and I was all excited. I opened the stomach, and the gut contents got everywhere. I wish I had removed the arms and legs first, as I would then have been able to eat some of the meat."
4. **Vacuum seal.** It reduces rancidity in both dried and frozen foods, and it forestalls freezer burn. Store dried meat either in the freezer (preferable), or in a cool, dark place.

Beware of Porcupine Quills
Due to their slowness, porcupines are common roadkill fare. Be very careful when processing, so that you do not get any quills in the meat. If you were to eat a quill, it could kill you by piercing a vital organ. Native people will often burn off the quills before butchering, and I do the same.

Other Sources for Wild Game

If roadkill is not an option for you, or if you want to augment what you find, try these ideas:

- Taxidermists
- Hunters and trappers
- Pelt fleshers
- Town and county road crews
- Contracted roadkill disposers
- Game wardens
- Wildlife preserve managers
- Farmers
- Nuisance animal controllers
- Local law enforcement agencies

Most of these individuals and agencies routinely dispose of every animal they get. Some people who hunt mainly for sport do not eat their kills, or they might end up with surplus. Trappers routinely dispose of their animals, as they are only interested in the pelts.

Even so, hardly any of these animals are available just for the asking. Many officials strictly follow policy, which usually means the carcasses are either taken to a disposal site or taken to a zoo for animal food. And people in general shy away from what they consider to be odd requests from strangers, particularly in this case where there may be legalities involved.

How, then, does one get in on the supply line? It is all about building relationship. My family and the staff I work with have taken advantage of all of the above sources, by getting to know the people involved and developing trusting relationships. When we ask agencies for hides to use in our tanning classes, we are routinely given the whole animal. Although we request only fat and bones from taxidermists for craft purposes, we are sometimes given meat as well. Once a year we bring these people an attractive goodies basket and/or send thank-you cards.

If you explain that you want to learn skinning and animal processing, and that you are looking for carcasses to practice on, you will get some positive results. Bring along the book, handout, or internet printout that you are learning from, and you will get even better results.

CHAPTER 6

Feasting Protocol

We may not be competing with vultures and coyotes for our share of the kill, yet we would do well to follow a feasting protocol, just as they do. Each of them has favorite parts that they go for first, if they have the option, and they have parts that they leave for last. The ultimate reason is nutrition; in a long-term survival situation, we want to maximize our nutritional intake as well.

There are two additional important considerations: rate of spoilage and preservation. We need to extract every edible calorie from the carcass that we can, as we probably won't know how long it will be until we come across another smorgasbord so bountiful. Taking nutrition, spoilage, and preservation into consideration, here is the most practical order of consumption.

Sequence for Consuming a Carcass
First: Blood
The most perishable and hardest-to-store component of an animal is the blood, so it makes sense to consume it first. Other than as an ethnic food, most Westerners are not accustomed to eating blood in any form. However throughout most of the world, blood either fresh, congealed, or as a component of soups, sausages, and stir-fries, is normal fare.

As nourishing as blood is—18% protein by weight, 170 calories per 8-ounce cup (orange juice has 120, whole milk has 150)—it is too high in iron and potassium to safely consume in quantity for any length of time. Although many people can drink a pint of blood, some can only hold down a cupful. Which is good, as overconsumption can lead to protein poisoning (see *Fifth: Flesh* later in this chapter). Mixing blood with other foods, which is the typical way it is consumed in most cultures, makes it more palatable.

To Collect the Blood

- **If the heart is still beating**, hang her upside down, sever the jugular vein and carotid artery on both sides of the neck, and catch the blood in a container.
- **If the animal is already dead**, very little will drain from the neck, even though the blood is fresh and not coagulated. Instead, open the chest cavity, sever the large vessels around the heart, and catch what runs out. Empty the blood from the heart. If there is an internal injury, scoop up the blood that has pooled around it.

Blood is a prime disease vector, so the animal must pass every test in chapter 4 in order to consider its blood safe to consume raw. To sterilize blood, follow the same guidelines as for meat.

To Gauge the Edibility of Blood

- **Bright red and runny** (or dark red not yet exposed to air) and metallic smelling means fresh and edible.
- **Coagulated** yet still fresh smelling means edible.
- **Crusted over** yet fresh smelling means questionable. Cook before eating.
- **Sour or rank smell** means inedible.

Second: The Head

The richness of organs, glands, and muscles in the head makes it the most nourishing and delicious part of the animal. And the second-most perishable and hard-to-store part of the animal. For these reasons, the Dene and Cree of northern Canada eat the head first, and they serve it as a delicacy to their guests. When the hunters come in fatigued at the end of the day, the first thing the women do is roast the caribou or moose head over the fire for them. My family serves the head first as well, and in survival situations, we consume the head right along with the blood.

Several years ago we were honored with a visit from John Danttouze, past chief of the Northland Dene in LacBrochet, Manitoba, which is just west of Churchill on Hudson Bay. John told us about his people's relationship with the Caribou (known to them as *Et-then*), which is so close that they call themselves *the Caribou People*.

When the weather turned cold, Jon said that his band would hunt the Caribou as they migrated southward in vast herds from the tundra into the sheltering taiga forest. When someone killed the first Caribou, they would have a Thanksgiving feast right on the spot. Making a great fire, they would heat rocks to place inside the Caribou's body cavity, which cooked the animal from the inside out.

In the meantime, the head would be roasted over the fire. Here is their method, which is the same one I teach in my classes.

Roasted Caribou Head

1. **Skewer the head** on a stick by shoving it through the nose and into the sinuses.
2. **Pierce the eyes** so they do not explode.
3. **Suspend the head** over a bed of hardwood coals.
4. **Rotate periodically** until all the hair burns off and the skin turns brown and crusty.
5. **Scrape off the crust**, which is actually the charred grain and epidermis.
6. **Re-suspend** over the coals, letting it slowly roast.
7. **Strip off jaw and head muscles** when cooked through, along with tongue, nose and eyes.
8. **Remove jawbone** and re-suspend to finish cooking through.

9. **Clean the remaining meat** and connective tissue from the skull, then crack the skull to extract the brain and sinus tissue.

This method works best for heads the size of cougar, coyote, and larger. Smaller heads can be skewered and roasted through right away. All they need is periodic rotation and a scraping.

Third: Internal Organs

Storehouses of a wide spectrum of nutrients, the organs are the most important sources of nourishment from the carcass. Along with fat, they are the cornerstones of a long-term carcass-based survival diet. The sheer volume of organ meat that a large carcass can provide makes the organs even more valuable.

When most of us hear *edible organs*, we think heart, liver, and maybe kidneys. In survival jargon—and in most of the world other than our corner—edible organs include everything in the chest cavity except for the gallbladder and stomach-gut contents (yet even they can be eaten when necessary).

Edible Organs

- Liver
- Heart
- Lungs
- Stomach(s)
- Spleen
- Diaphragm
- Sweetbreads (Thymus Gland)
- Testicles

- Ovaries
- Mammary glands
- Pancreas
- Kidneys
- Veins and arteries
- Connective tissue
- Intestines
- Bladder

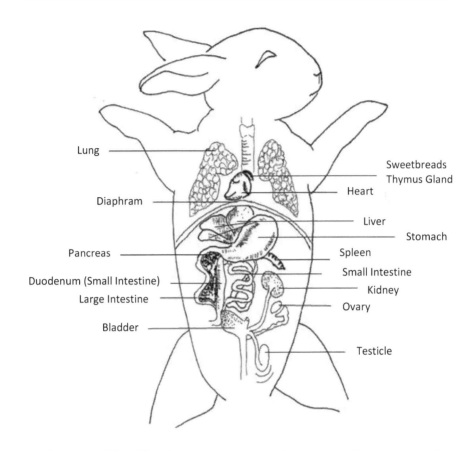

Learn to identify, clean, prepare, and preserve these organs by practicing on roadkill, hunted, or domestic animals. Following are the most important processing tips.

Organ Processing
- **Liver.** First, check out the health of the liver according to the guidelines on page 13. Next, remove the gallbladder, a small thumb-shaped gland attached to the liver. It contains bile, a bitter-tasting liquid that aids in fat digestion. Getting it on anything could render the meat inedible. Pinch the duct connecting liver to gallbladder, then gently tear or cut it off. Keep pulling gently, to remove the bile duct that runs to the small intestine.

Members of the deer family do not have gallbladders, nor do members of the horse, llama, and camel clans.

- **Intestines.** Cut into short lengths, turn inside out, and wash thoroughly. They are then ready to be cooked and eaten. Or you may further process the sections and use them for pemmican or rendered fat storage (see next chapter). Scrape the slimy surface off with a split branch or the backside of your knife, tie one end off, fill up loosely with dry grass, and hang up to dry.
- **Stomach.** Turn inside out and scrub thoroughly. If the taste bothers you, cook slowly in water until edible.
- **Bladder.** Turn inside out and rinse. It can be eaten like intestines and stomach, yet may be more valuable to use as a storage container. Pat dry, blow up like a balloon, tie off openings, and hang to dry.
- **All other organs** need no special attention. Prepare and eat any way you choose, as long as you assess their condition and edibility (see pages 11-13) and follow the cooking guidelines.

When You Have Too Much

Store organs and fresh flesh for as long as possible, and then cook through to extend their shelf life. With the bacteria killed and a cool, dry, fly-proof storage area, you could forestall spoilage by a couple of days. A thorough reheating might give another day.

Fourth: Fat

When it comes to long-term survival, the importance of fat cannot be overstated. The availability of calories is the determining factor in most long-term survival situations. We can have the tools and we can have the know-how, yet without the energy to implement them, they do us no good. Fat is such a vitally important component of a sustainable survival effort that oftentimes only fat and organs will be taken from a carcass.

Determining the edibility of subcutaneous and organ fats has already been covered, as has the procurement of invisible fat. In the next chapter, we will learn how to render, store, and consume fat, from both fish and mammals, in the most efficient way.

It is important to remember that animal carcasses are not our only fat source. The forthcoming full-sized book which was referenced in the Introduction will show us where we need to go when a kill is not available.

As precious as fat can be in a survival situation, consuming too much can lead to problems. Fortunately, we have a built-in shut-off switch, in the form of revulsion for fat when we try to eat more than we can properly metabolize. We start feeling nauseous and headachy, with the mere smell or sight of fat turning our stomach. Even thinking about fat can do it.

Overconsumption can lead to vomiting, intestinal cramps, and diarrhea. Thanks to both our shut-off switch and our bodily reactions, it is hard to over consume to the point of causing ourselves serious harm. Our shut-off switch adjusts to our caloric needs, which can vary greatly with climate, season, and activity level. An Inuit's winter diet can consist of almost half fat, and recently a woman crossed Antarctica on foot, fueling herself on pure olive oil.

Fifth: Flesh

As you now know, the importance of meat in long-term survival and wilderness living situations is overrated by the majority of people. The belief is so ingrained that it has caused the unnecessary suffering and death of numerous explorers, homesteaders, trappers, plane crash, and shipwreck survivors. The emphasis on low-fat diets over the past thirty years has only further entrenched this belief.

Compounding all of that is the fact that in an extreme survival situation, we are often not able to think clearly. In the year-long wilderness survival trainings I run, some students will get the notion that when foraging for edible plants, fruit, and insects is not going well, all they have to do to compensate is increase their consumption of meat.

Before long they find themselves continually hungry, even though they have full bellies. They complain of having no energy, oftentimes along with a continual headache, and they have *ketone breath*, which smells like nail polish or overripe pineapple. What has happened to them?

The maximum amount of meat per day that the average adult can safely metabolize on a consistent basis is ten to thirteen ounces. The amount will vary with gender, age, and activity level. When our meat consumption exceeds 45% of caloric intake, we exceed our liver and kidneys' ability to process out the byproducts of protein breakdown. Excess levels of uric acid (which may lead to gout) and calcium oxalate (the mineral which forms kidney stones) build up in the bloodstream. An overload of ketones, byproducts of fat breakdown, can cause kidney damage. The condition is commonly known as *protein poisoning* or *rabbit starvation*.

It is referred to as rabbit starvation, because in the wintertime in the Northcountry, rabbits are often the only easily available protein. Their meat is very lean, so people trying to survive on it put themselves on the low-fat, high protein diet that quickly leads to protein poisoning. And that is just what happens to many who are new at living off of the wilds.

Even though it is called rabbit starvation, it is not just rabbit flesh that causes it. In the wintertime, most animals grow lean from burning their fat to keep warm. In my area, deer meat contributes most to protein poisoning, followed by snowshoe hares (who are technically not rabbits, yet the term *rabbit poisoning* originates with them).

Protein Poisoning Symptoms

Short-Term Symptoms	**Long-Term Symptoms**

Short-Term Symptoms
1 to 3 weeks
- Nausea
- Fatigue
- Headache
- Diarrhea
- Insatiable hunger

Long-Term Symptoms
- Constipation
- Low heart rate
- Low blood pressure
- Joint pain

After the onset of protein poisoning, death can result in as little as a few weeks. Contributing factors usually include nutrient deficiencies, weather extremes, isolation, and/or injury.

The Cure
- **Fast.** If lean meat is the only food available, fasting may be necessary in order to restore metabolic function and forestall death. With increased functioning, other options may become possible.
- **Increase fat intake.** Symptoms in mild cases can abate quickly when dietary fat is increased to 55% or more of caloric intake. Reducing protein intake alone has little or no effect.

Fortunately, protein poisoning is rare in the Northcountry, as nearly everyone is aware of it and takes preventative measures. Most cases occur in survival situations and with people new to subsistence living.

All of this is not to diminish the importance of meat as a dietary protein source, but rather to point out the folly of relying on meat as the primary source of calories. In a long-term survival or wilderness living situation, *the problem is often not too little meat, but too much*. Knowing that, you can make informed decisions when carcasses are plentiful, one of which may be to throw away the meat and keep the other parts of the animal.

> **Practice Now**
> The next chapter shows how to prepare meat in a way that will actually contribute to our long-term survival. Take it seriously by practicing the skill now. Old beliefs die hard, so if we do not imprint the awareness needed in survival situations, the odds are that when we are stressed and desperate, we will resort to the old and familiar. This means that we could end up killing ourselves and others for no reason.

Sixth: Skin and Bones

You may have heard of people boiling old bones, skins, or leather in a last-ditch effort to stay alive. I have come across accounts in historical novels and movies that were no-doubt romanticized, and I have seen reports in the historical record, some of which were probably exaggerated as well. Yet there is a factual basis for looking to skin and bones as survival foods.

Imagine coming across a kill site, and all we see are some scattered bones and scraps of skin. Lament not, as those benevolent scavengers have left the best for last. Wolves go for the large marrow-containing bones as soon as they are reachable, and hyenas, with their powerful jaws and bone-crushing teeth, are specialized marrow scavengers. The Old World's bearded vulture, a great bird with a wingspan sometimes over nine feet, lets smaller vultures strip a carcass. She then comes in to grab a femur bone, which she takes up to a great height and drops on rocks below. The bone shatters, leaving her the marrow to easily devour.

Why such a preference for marrow? Because it is some of the most life-sustaining food there is. A bearded vulture's diet is comprised of up to 90% marrow, and in a survival situation, we would be wise to follow her example and grab a couple of rocks and get cracking. Even if the bones have been laying there for weeks, the marrow could still be good if there were the ideal dry and cool weather conditions.

Marrow: A True Food of Last Resort
Marrow is the last fat reserve an animal draws upon. She may be old or emaciated, yet have succulent marrow. Many starving people have passed up sorry looking carcasses, not knowing that the animal's food of last resort was still there for them.

There are two types of marrow: red and yellow. The red, which is found primarily in flat bones such as the pelvis and ribs, produces blood cells and platelets, and it contains a significant amount of fat. In the next chapter I'll explain how to process red marrow. Right here we are focusing on yellow marrow, which is found in the large leg bones. With a mere 3 ounces containing 450 to 750 calories (which is 15% to 25% of adult daily need), along with six grams of protein (around 10% of daily need) and significant amounts of iron, phosphorus, and other nutrients, yellow marrow is a powerhouse we cannot afford to pass up.

On top of that, it comes ready to eat: just crack open the bone and slip out the creamy column of sweet and nutty flavored nourishment. There are three prerequisites.

Before Eating the Marrow
- **Check the species** to see if its meat and fat can be eaten raw (see *When Raw Is Safe* box on page 45).
- **Wash and heat-sterilize** the bone surface before cracking when there is risk of marrow contamination.
- **Determine edibility** by running the marrow through the fat assessment on page 18.

And now for those dried-up scraps of skin, which are another often-overlooked food source when survival is at stake. Again, we need to work through our old mindsets now in order to establish the new eating patterns that could someday save our lives. Otherwise when the pressure is on and we are not thinking clearly, we will not be able to see beyond the old and familiar, and we will skip right over potential food sources. That old skin may not resemble the type of food we would expect to keep us alive, and it may not be an energy goldmine like marrow, yet it will sustain us. With 3 ounces of your average bird or mammal skin providing around 300 calories, which includes about 15 grams of protein, we could live on it for a while if we needed to. As a bonus, there are often additional calories in the form of subcutaneous fat still attached to the skin.

Oftentimes, scavengers and predators will tear the skin off of an animal, both to get at the more nourishing flesh and organs, and to get rid of the fur and feathers. That is a boon for us, as the skin will not rot with the remainder of the carcass. In sunny weather the skin could actually dry out and remain preserved. Even when the whole carcass is consumed, there are usually patches of edible skin lying around. Comb the area, as the scraps could have been dragged around as playthings, or by small scavengers.

Let's say we found a few pieces of tough rawhide covered with scruffy fur. They look anything but edible, yet we are going to transform them into something not only nourishing, but tasty.

To Prepare Skin for Eating
1. **Soak in clean water** until soft and fully rehydrated. Change water and rinse skin often.
2. **Assess for edibility** using the criteria in Chapter 4.
3. **Search for scent/poison glands** and cut them out. Get to know your animals, as gland locations and toxicity vary widely among species. American deer, for example, have glands on rear legs, forehead, in front of eyes, and between toes. Many amphibians exude poison through their skin. Experienced outdoors people and butchers

can be valuable resources, and there is much online and printed information available.

4. **Remove hair/feathers**, using one of these methods:

- **Pluck.** Works best for feathers. Anchor the skin and pull feathers in the direction they lay. If it proves too difficult, go to next procedure.

- **Scald.** For both feathers and hair: make sure skin is well hydrated, drench with water heated to 160° (which is uncomfortable to the touch, but not steaming), then attempt plucking. If the hair/feathers are not slipping, drench again.

- **Burn and scrape.** With an open flame, quickly sear the hair/feathers off of the skin, taking care not to cook it. Scrape off the charred stubble.

- **Shave.** Works best for hair. Hold the skin taut and scrape it at a right angle with a sharp knife. If the hair is too tough to shave, try cutting it off at skin level.

- **Cook with hair on.** This is the desperation method, and it may or may not work. Hair and feathers can slip after the skin is softly cooked. When it is baked, plucking often tears skin apart.

5. **Cook.** Most skin is too tough to eat without cooking, even if it is from an animal that is safe to eat raw. Cooking breaks down connective tissue and improves digestibility. Some skins will respond best to one cooking method, and some to another, so experiment with boiling, baking, roasting, and frying. Thin-slice or dice up the toughest skins, and cook them long and slow. Hint: when a skin gets too dry and tough to eat from roasting on an open fire, soak to soften and roast again. Or use the method in the following box.

> **Ground Down**
> The !Kung, hunter-gatherers of South Africa's Kalahari Desert, relish the taste of skin. They dry it and pound it up for cooking, and they do the same with gristle. (Lee and DeVore 1976)

Skin dries, stores, and packs easily. When you have extra, clean it, scrape off the fat, and dry it in the sun or over coals. You can then cut it down and pack it in storage containers, or just hang it in a cool, dry place. Watch for skin-eating bugs.

CHAPTER 7

Pemmican: Superfood for the Long Haul

In a long-term survival or wilderness living situation, we need a way to preserve, store, and easily transport the meat and fat from a large carcass (or from a pile of fish—see next chapter) that we can't completely consume before it spoils. We cannot afford to abandon it, as we have no guarantee of when—or even if—we will again come by such a bonanza.

Fortunately for us, the Northcountry Indians solved our dilemma by developing a concentrated mixture of protein and fat that is lightweight, long lasting, and made entirely from a carcass. The Cree and Ojibwe call this high-energy fast food *pemmican*, which means *rendering fat*. There couldn't be a more appropriate name, as fat, the ultimate source of life-sustaining calories, is the most important ingredient.

The early explorers and fur traders were quick to adopt pemmican, and people still use it on backpacking canoeing trips. Its undying popularity rests on the fact that it is a whole food that can be lived on exclusively for a year or more if need be. The physicians who supervised a year-long all meat-and-fat diet trial stated in their conclusion that people "may subsist on an exclusive meat diet in a temperate climate without damage to health or efficiency." Reported in Time Magazine (March 31, 1930), Canadian ethnologist Vilhjalmur Stefansson, who participated in the experiment, commented at its conclusion: "I am wide awake and am more aggressive in my work than I was before I started this test." What more could one ask of a survival food?

Making Pemmican

We are already familiar with pemmican, as it is nothing more than a simple sausage. Pemmican is made from only two ingredients: meat and fat. Think of the process as separating, and then reuniting, these two major components of the carcass. The meat and fat are processed differently, each in the way that best preserves it. Traditionally, lean meat from ungulates such as Bison, Elk, Deer, and Moose is used, along with lard (semi-solid rendered fat). Any fat-free meat can be used, and nearly any fat works.

Before we get into the process, we need to clear up a misconception that could prove fatal if left unaddressed: smoking preserves meat. When at all possible, most Natives dry meat (including fish) with just sun and wind. The reason is simple: it works. They have to rely entirely on the food they prepare, and it sometimes needs to carry them through a season or more before they can replenish their supplies. When supplemental fire is needed because of unfavorable drying conditions, any smoke flavoring the meat picks up is incidental to the drying process. With some Native people, smoky meat reflects negatively upon the skill of the dryer.

Is There Any Benefit to Smoking?

Smoking may keep some meats from spoiling for a few days to a week. However, by sealing in moisture, heavy smoking could actually help meat rot, along with creating the anaerobic conditions for botulism and other bacterial killers (see pages 13-16).

So where did the smoke-preservation myth arise? In the Americas and Europe, many old-time smoke houses were kept smoky to keep flies off of meat during the salt-curing process. The ham and bacon ended up tasting smoky, so consumers started to assume that smoke was the curing agent. Over time, smoked food became an acculturated taste, and today many foods only have added smoke flavoring.

The Eight-Step Process

Step 1: Remove Meat and Fat from Carcass.

Following the edibility guidelines in chapter 4, select only the prime cuts. *Anything that is contaminated or showing rot could ruin the batch.* All fat is suitable, and the best meat comes from the large, lean muscles of the legs, along with the tenderloins and backstraps. Remove the muscles whole, and set them aside for slicing in step 3. The Indians were always careful not to cut the muscles across the grain, as they would then fall apart and be difficult to slice. Keep all edible materials from touching the ground.

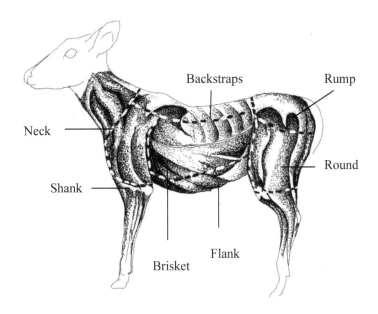

Step 2: Separate and Clean.

Fat and meat need to be processed separately, because if there is any fat in the meat during drying, the meat could spoil. As well, the temperature needed to render fat would destroy most of the meat's nutritional value. Separate processing gives two stable products that, when mixed, have optimal keeping quality. Thoroughly rinse fat and meat if they show any contamination, and allow them to drip dry. Trim off flesh with embedded dirt, and remove foreign objects such as sticks and bone fragments. Be meticulous in trimming all fat and connective tissue from meat.

Step 3: Dry the Meat.

Drying takes longer than rendering, so get the drying process started, then render. It takes about 5 pounds of fresh meat to make 1 pound of dry meat.

1. **Choose a warm, dry, sunny day**—if you have the option—and start early to take full advantage of available drying time.
2. **Slice meat** across the grain as thin as possible—1/4 inch or less is ideal—to speed drying time. Getting it dry in one day is the goal, as we are in a race with maggots, rot, and changing weather. Hint: freeze the meat if you can, as partially frozen meat is easy to slice thin. Below-freezing nights and warm days are ideal.
3. **Hang slices** on a drying rack in full breeze and sunlight. The branches of a fallen tree work well. The higher the better, as humidity drops with elevation. Avoid low areas, which are typically humidity pockets.

4. **Test for dryness** by bending several of the larger pieces at their thickest spots. If rubbery, they need more drying time; if brittle and crack easily, they are done. *Do not compromise on this step.* Here is an accounting from one of our students: "Earlier this summer in Sweden, a batch of my jerky turned moldy due to damp drying conditions." In a survival situation that story could have meant his life.

When dry, pack away immediately in an airtight container so they do not reabsorb moisture. If they are not completely dry a couple of hours before sunset, pack away to avoid evening humidity.

1. **Use supplemental fire** if conditions are not ideal for drying or weather changes. Radiant heat from a bed of coals dries better than direct flame. Place a stick A-frame over the fire, with the meat slices draped over the horizontals. Manage the fire for a warm, drying air current, but not too warm that it cooks the meat.

2. **Roast the meat.** *Warning: skip this step and risk a Trichinosis infection* (see pages 15 and 16), as dried meat is one of the primary infective agents. The infection is easily rendered harmless by raising the meat's temperature to 160°. However, we have no guarantee that our primitive drying method achieved a sustained 160°. We must take one of these two options:

   - **Pan fry**. Bring the dried meat to the point where it is too hot to hold, for three minutes. When there is neither pan nor fire, try heating flat, black rocks in direct sunlight.
   - **Roast** on hot coals, to the point where the meat is too hot to hold, for three minutes.

What we have created here is *jerky*, which can be stored and consumed as-is—with other foods. Remember that meat is not a complete food, so do not try to live on it, even in a survival situation.

> **When Raw Is Safe**
> If the animal is a vegetarian and has passed the cause-of-death and edibility tests in chapter 4, her meat and fat are probably safe to eat raw. However there are no guarantees, as the animal could still harbor unknown pathogens. Even the most dedicated vegetarian animal might eat meat, particularly when suffering from nutritional deficiencies.

Step 4: Pulverize the Meat.
Immediately after roasting, the jerky is at its crispest and will pulverize the easiest. Place several pieces at a time in a depression in a large stone and use a comfortable-to-grip hammer stone to crush it into cornmeal  consistency. Choose hard, fine-grained stones that will not create grit. Bag immediately after pulverizing.

Step 5: Render the Fat.
Animal fat is actually specialized cellular tissue that stores fat globules. Traditional rendering methods utilize either rot or heat to rupture the cells, which releases the liquid fat. Following are the four common methods:

- **Hang in the sun.** Incorporating both heat and rotting, this is the easiest method of all, as it takes minimal effort, requires no equipment, and creates very little mess. There is some waste, as not all the fat gets rendered. Just hang a slab of fat (the thinner, the better) or small, fatty, skinned and gutted animal(s) in the sun above a collection  vessel. If you do not have one, improvise by lining a depression in the ground with a hide. Accelerate the process by placing flat, dark rocks behind the fat-collecting vessel to absorb and radiate solar energy.

Variation: use fire as a heat source in cold weather or when there is no sun.

- **Rot.** A favorite with the Inuit, it works best with small oil-producing animals such as fish, yet it can be used for slabs of oil-containing fat from larger animals. Fill a container and let sit covered but unsealed in a warm place. Periodically skim the oil off the top.

- **Fry.** Dice the fat—the smaller the better—and fry, stirring frequently, until it becomes crisp and porous. Strain or decant to separate the liquid from the cracklings (which are nourishing and edible). Use low heat and be careful of overcooking: watch for the fat caramelizing and cracklings turning brown. Overheated fat can be damaging to your health, and it does not keep well.

Caution: Hot Fat Can Cause Serious Burns
and it is extremely combustible. Remove immediately from fire at first sign of smoking. Remain present at all times when the fat is cooking, and be careful not to drip any fat onto the fire.

- **Boil.** Prepare as for frying, and then boil in an equal part of water, skimming the liquid fat off the top. A Cheyenne method of extracting fat from greasy bones and those containing red marrow is to crack them up, boil them, and tilt the pot to blow the grease off the top of the water.

Our final product will be either *lard*, which is semisolid at room temperature, or *oil*, which remains liquid at room temperature. Lard is the best product for pemmican, though oil can be used. Quality lard in the amount needed comes mainly from ungulates. Wolf and Coyote provide exceptional lard, but in very small quantity.

Unlike raw fat, lard and oil will not easily spoil if properly stored. Along with sterilizing, rendering removes spoiling contaminants and converts fat to a liquid form, which is much more easily and safely stored than fat. It can be kept for years in completely filled, sealed containers kept in a cold, dark place.

Even in less-than-ideal conditions, well-prepared oil and lard have impressive keeping qualities. I recently came across a bag of lard that I had placed on a shelf in the garage three years ago, and its center was still fresh-smelling and edible.

Saving Bad Lard

The purer the lard, the longer the pemmican's shelf life. Clarify lard clouded from old blood or other foreign matter by adding it to an equal amount of water and heating almost to the boiling point, while continually stirring. Do not boil, to keep fat from spattering and burning. Most foreign matter will be either water soluble or heavier than fat, so it will settle down into the water. When the fat is clarified, decant or ladle it off.

Step 6: Combine Meat and Lard.

Knead thoroughly together in a ratio of two parts meat to one part lard. Protein provides four calories per gram and fat gives nine, which along with dried meat being around 80% protein and lard being nearly 100% fat, gives this pemmican a caloric profile of 40% from protein and 60% from fat, which many nutritionists consider to be ideal for active people.

But Where is the Fruit?

Many of us expect pemmican to contain fruit. The Indians would sometimes mix dried blueberries, cranberries, currants, or other fruit with dried meat for a children's treat, or for ceremonial pemmican. However, standard pemmican was just meat and fat. My hunch is that for the brisk frontier pemmican trade, the Indians produced a flavored product in an attempt to imitate the sausages their non-native clients were accustomed to, and that is what we have come to know as pemmican.

Step 7: Pack in Airtight Containers.

Fill containers completely, compressing to remove all air. Seal the container, taking care not to trap any air inside. For containers that do not self-seal, cap with a ½ inch layer of the firmest lard you have, which is the least likely to melt during storage. For a long shelf life, pemmican must remain sealed from air, moisture, and insects.

Pint to quart-size containers work well. Fabricate containers from the trachea, stomach, heart sac, bladder, intestines (which sausage casings are made from), pieces of rawhide, the leg-sock sections of a hide, and the skins of small animals. Refer back to page 31 for how to prepare stomach, bladder, and intestines for eating, which are also the same methods used for creating storage containers.

To make a rawhide pouch: wet the hide to soften, form to desired shape, fill with an absorbent material such as crumbled punky wood, and set out to dry.

Resting on the satisfaction of a beautiful final product, some of us will be tempted to cut corners on this step and the next. We cannot afford to do so, and risk our all-important survival food not being there when we need it for ourselves and our loved ones.

Step 8: Store.

The ideal storage space is cold, pitch black, dry, and free of vermin. The closer we get to that, the longer our pemmican is going to last. In cold weather, nearly any dark, secure place will suffice. Hang containers high, to keep them both dry and out of reach. In warm weather, look for caves, deep crevasses, and old dens. Check periodically for insect infestation, animal depredation, and spoilage. For travel, pack containers in dry grass or moss, in order to cushion, insulate, and protect them from moisture.

Quickie Pemmican

When time is at a premium, as is often the case in a survival situation—and when we do not have prime ingredients, here is a recipe that will produce serviceable pemmican. It may not have the keeping qualities of better-made pemmican, and it may not be quite as nourishing, yet who is going to quibble over such details when life is at stake?

I came across the process in an interview with an elder Crow woman from the 1800s named Pretty-shield. The whole process can be completed in a day.

Step 1: Prepare Meat.

Slice across the grain, as thin as possible.

Step 2: Air Dry.

But only to the point that the surface is dry and the meat begins to shrink.

Step 3: Roast.

Hang close to the fire to brown and drive out all moisture.

Step 4: Pulverize.

Same as step 4 under *The Eight-Step Process*.

Step 5: Render Fat.

Break up marrow-containing bones, boil, and skim grease off the top.

Step 6: Combine Meat and Grease, pour into containers, and let harden.

Eat Wisely

Pemmican is a concentrated high-energy food, which can be a curse as well as a blessing. To get the most out of it and keep from getting sick:

- Use as a primary source of nourishment only when actively living outdoors. The calorie-protein load is too excessive for sedentary or sporadically active people.
- Consume only about one quarter of your normal food volume.
- Chew well.

Keep well hydrated, as water is needed for the breakdown of fat and protein. However, do not drink while eating or soon after, or you will dilute digestive acids.

CHAPTER 8

Fish Pemmican: The Little-known Superfood

This chapter details the entire fish pemmican-making process. It will show you how to find the amount of fish needed to produce a long-lasting food that is super-rich in calories, protein, vitamins, and minerals. In some regions of the country, particularly along the coasts and during spawning runs, quantities of fish are more available than large animal carcasses. Having the skill to process and convert both land-animal meat and fish into pemmican greatly increases our odds of long-term survival, along with our ability to live sustainably in the farther places.

I learned to rely on the great numbers of seasonally available fish from the Ojibwe and Menominee Indians of my area, whose traditional diet is based on fish. When hunting and trapping does not go well, they know fish will carry them through. I also learned much from the other animals. Nearly everyone knows that bears, eagles, wolves, and others are right there to take advantage of spawning runs and fish die-offs. At one time, the native people participated as well, and in some areas the tradition lives on. How do they know when and where the fish are to be found?

How to Find Fish in Abundance
- **Floods.** When floodwaters recede, fish often get trapped in pools that gradually dry up on them. Find the pools and collect the dead and dying fish.
- **Drought.** Similar to floods: drying-up lakes, rivers, and ponds concentrate their fish populations, which end up dying en masse from warming water and asphyxiation.

- **Spawning runs** usually occur up streams or along beaches in spring or autumn, depending on species. Learn the spawning habits of the species in areas you frequent.
- **Freeze-outs.** Shallow, heavily vegetated bodies of water will sometimes become oxygen-starved when they are frozen over and snow-covered. Without sun penetration to encourage oxygenation from photosynthesis, fish begin to asphyxiate. In an effort to breathe, fish will often crowd into open-water inlets, where they can be scooped up. Or chop a hole in the ice to create the same effect.
- **Circling or excited birds** along shorelines and riverbanks. Concentrations of fish draw seagulls, eagles, ravens, and crows, who can often be seen from a distance.
- **Agitated sounds.** When cover is heavy, we may be able to hear the hubbub of a feeding frenzy before seeing it.
- **Fresh and well-used animal trails** leading to water. When a die-off or spawning run is on, scavengers and predators can wear in a trail that leads us right to the site.
- **Fish remains and scat.** Most scavengers and predators are sloppy eaters, and you will see their scat splattered on rocks and piled on the shoreline. Finding such a sign in the daytime could mean the run will be on again that night.
- **Local knowledge.** It can take years to become familiar with any area's spawning, flood, and freeze-out cycles. Jumpstart the process by talking with longtime residents who already know.

Let's say we found forty dead catfish in the shrinking pools of a dried-up riverbed. How do we tell if they are safe to either eat or process into pemmican? Fish meat is in a class by itself, as it deteriorates rapidly in comparison with the flesh of mammals. At the same time, factors such as temperature and sunlight play into the condition of any flesh. Here are the edibility signs unique to fish:

- **Odor.** Contrary to popular belief, fish do not normally smell fishy. When the odor appears, it is a sign that their flesh is starting to break down.
- **Eyes.** The eye lenses of most fish look dark when they are alive, and they gradually turn white after death. However, a white lens alone is not enough reason to reject a fish.
- **Color.** Many fish have brightly colored spots or distinctive patterns, and some have silvery, reflective scales. A freshly killed fish retains these features for only a short time before they start to dull, and then turn opaque or milky looking.
- **Stiffness.** As with mammals and birds, rigor mortis will set in at some point after a fish has died, and it can persist for a long time under the right conditions. It starts at the tail and works its way toward the head. As with other animals, onset is fast with fatigued fish. Rigor mortis in fish usually starts at the tail, and the muscles stiffen gradually along the body toward the head
- **Flesh Tone.** This is the defining factor as to whether or not a fish is edible. With most fresh fish, the flesh will bounce back after you stick your finger into it. However when the flesh starts to break down, it will get mushy and your finger impression will remain. (Note: take into account that some fish are softer fleshed than others. Practice is needed in order to reliably conduct this test.)

When a fish fails any two of the first four tests, go directly to *Flesh Tone*. If the fish fails only one of the first four, it is likely in good enough condition to eat. However when there is any doubt, do the Flesh Tone test.

If our fish tests out as inedible, we still have to get as much nourishment out of them as we can. When our life is at stake, we cannot afford to pass up any source of sustenance. Fortunately, fish oil is relatively stable, and we might be able to process it out of the otherwise-unusable fish.

Salvaging Inedible Fish
1. **Cut out a section of belly flesh** between the gills and the anal fin, including the pelvic fins (see illustration). With many species, the bellies are rich in oil.

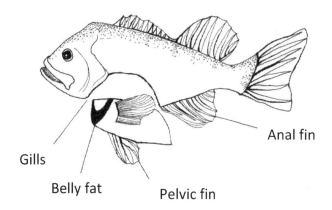

Anal fin

Gills

Belly fat   Pelvic fin

2. **Pinch and roll it between your fingers** to see if it is oily. If so,
3. **Determine edibility** by using the *Fat Edibility Assessment* on page 18. If it passes,
4. **Cut out and smoke the bellies** over a smudge fire (see step 4 on page 59).
5. **Extract the oil,** either by frying and pouring off the oil, or by roasting over coals and catching the drips.

We can also salvage the oil from the skins and heads of fatty fish that predators and scavengers have left behind. When fish are plentiful, bears will often eat just the skin, and wolves will take just the heads. And there are the skins and heads resulting from our fish processing for pemmican. All we have to do is put the fish parts in a pot, cover them with water and bring them to a boil, then skim the rendered oil off the top.

> **No Pot? No Problem.**
> In a survival situation, we may well find ourselves with no cookware. Or we may have chosen to cook primitively during our wilderness living experience. Here is how to boil:
> 1. **Find a hollow log** or rock depression that will hold water, or dig a hole and line it with a fresh hide.
> 2. **Add fish parts** and cover with water.
> 3. **Heat rocks,** fist-size or a little smaller, in a fire. To minimize the chance of exploding rocks and grit in your food, choose ones that are solid, round, fine-grained, and smooth, with no pits or cracks.
> 4. **Add a few rocks** to the water, replacing them as they cool.

The oil we produce can either be added directly to the pemmican we are making, or it can be stored for later use. Following are instructions for making an oil storage container such as used by the Ojibwe Indians of my area, and by many other natives. It also works well for fish pemmican and other purposes where a weatherproof container is needed.

Making a Fish-Skin Container

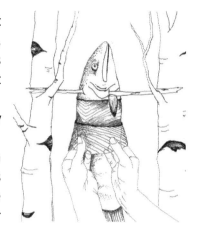

1. **Skin a large fish.** Starting at the head, cut skin from flesh, turning the skin inside out as you progress. Be careful not to cut through the skin.
2. **Clean the skin** by carefully removing all flesh and fat.
3. **Sew up holes,** using a baseball stitch for small holes and a whip stitch for large holes, and seal with conifer pitch.

Baseball Stitch   **Whip Stitch**

4. **Inflate to dry** by blowing up like a balloon or filling with dry grass.
5. **Fill with oil,** remove air, seal, and store in a cool, dark place, following the step 7-8 instructions on page 48.

Once we have usable fish, we then need to modify the red-meat processing method, in order to accommodate the unique properties of fish. The methods differ enough from each other that the Ojibwe use a special term for fish pemmican: *nooka'igan*, which translates to *dry, smoked fish*. The term is meaningful to me because I learned it along with the process, and I want to honor those who taught it to me by sharing the term with you. Yet for the sake of clarity, I suggest that we simply use *fish pemmican*.

The primary reason for the differences between the red meat and fish processes is that with fish it is difficult to separate fat from flesh. In order to do it successfully, much fat and flesh would be wasted, which is unacceptable when every calorie counts. For that reason, native people have developed three different methods for making fish pemmican: the *Smoke Method*, the *Cold Method*, and the *Hot Method*. In this chapter, we will be giving instructions for all three methods.

Generally speaking, the less oily the fish, the more suitable it is for drying. Yet the Indians developed a way to process the oil and flesh without having to separate them, which is known as the

Smoke Method. It can be made to work in all seasons, and in either wet or dry conditions.

To successfully use the process, it is important to understand that—contrary to popular belief—smoking does little to preserve meat. Maggots, mold, and bacteria seem to like the flavor of smoke just as much as we do. Here is the result of the first attempt of one of our students at drying fish: "While in Norway, we caught and smoke-dried a lot of trout, which we took with us when we left. We soon discovered that some of them weren't thoroughly dried and started molding."

With the Smoke Method, drying does the primary preserving work, with the smoke only contributing to keeping the oil from going rancid.

Fish pemmican is best made with oily fish, and that is what the Smoke Method is best suited for. In my area, suckers, whitefish, and cisco are the preferred species. Most large bodies of water have one or more species of oily fish.

To determine whether or not a fish is oily, use the pinch test just described under *Salvaging Inedible Fish*. For non-oily fish, skip ahead to *The Cold Method* or *The Hot Method*.

Unless we have access to a high-fat fish like the Northwest Coast's candle fish (also called *eulachon*, a Chinook Indian term), which during spawning can be 15% fat, the pemmican we produce will fall short of the ideal caloric profile of 40% from protein and 60% from fat. The fattiest fish that most of us have access to will produce a product that at best gives 45% of its calories from fat.

Trying to subsist on pemmican with that low a fat calorie percentage—or lower—puts us at risk of protein poisoning (see pages 31 and 32). We *must* either supplement with a non-protein caloric source or add fat to our pemmican. Oil extracted from inedible fish or fish parts (see page 54) can be used, along with any fat from other animals that we might have.

Following are the three methods for making fish pemmican.

The Smoke Method
Step 1: Gut and Behead.
Leave the skin on, as the fat is under the skin, and the skin keeps the fat from oxidizing and dripping during smoking. As the fat renders, the flesh absorbs it.

Step 2: Open Up.
Slice the fish in half vertically, to create two splits. You can leave the splits connected at the tail, back, or stomach, or you can separate them. Every inch or so, slash the splits transversely on the flesh side, almost through to the skin, to help release moisture.

Step 3: Pierce to Hang.
With sharp sticks, poke through the tail ends of the splits, so they will hang spread-out. The tail-connected splits can just be draped over the sticks.

Step 4: Suspend over Smudge Fire.

Arrange the splits side-by-side, like clothing hung in a closet, over a smoky, no-flame fire. To keep from cooking the fish or adding moisture, the smoke must be cool and dry. Leave enough room between the splits for adequate circulation.

Step 5: Cover with Bark Sheet.

Lay a bark sheet over the top of the fish to retain warmth, and use side panels as necessary. We are using the fire to create warmth and accelerated airflow, yet not enough heat to cook the fish.

Step 6: Drive out Remaining Moisture.

When the splits, broken open at the thickest part, are dry all the way through, remove them from the fire and immediately place them in a frying pan or on a hot rock to drive out any remaining moisture. The Ojibwe call the result *nameteg*, which means *dried fish*.

> **Warning**: some people over-process at this point because they mistake the oily feel of the flesh for water. To prevent moisture reabsorption, continue through the next steps without interruption.

Step 7: Break up and Debone.

The bones should now remove easily. If not, they have been over-processed. Try loosening the bones by gently crushing the splits with a hammer stone.

Step 8: Flake.

Bend splits to crumble the flesh and work it off of the skin. The texture does not have to be as fine as with red meat. Scrape any remaining flesh and oil off of the skin, and keep the skin to extract any residual oil from it (see page 54).

Step 9: Blend and Pack.

Add oil/lard if desired, mix thoroughly, and pack tightly into airtight pint-to-quart size containers. Be sure that all air has been compressed out.

Step 10: Store.

Place high in a cool, dark, dry place. Make sure the containers are beyond the reach of animals. Check periodically for damage and spoilage.

The next two methods work best for lean fish. They both require an outside source of fat in order to produce pemmican. Lean dried fish contain as little as 3% fat, and they range from 60 to 85% protein, which is comparable to dried red meat. We can then use the same two-parts-meat to one-part-fat formula as for red-meat pemmican, to create our desired caloric profile of 40% from protein and 60% from fat.

The Cold Method

The best drying temperature for this method is right around freezing. We need a breezy location that is out of the sun and protected from rain and snow, along with fairly consistent low humidity. The method requires a one-to-two month drying time. When this is not an option, as will be the case in some survival situations, skip this method and go to the next one: *The Hot Method*.

If the temperature rises much over 40°F for two days straight, especially early on when the splits still have high moisture content, they could begin to spoil. Abandon the Cold Method and finish the splits off with the Hot Method. Or bag the splits and put them on ice until the temperature drops.

Rising humidity along with a rise in temperature creates an even more critical situation. If the splits start to soften, they are reabsorbing moisture, and they must be either transferred to the Hot Method or bagged and put on ice until drying conditions improve. In regions where the humidity can rise in the evening, it might be necessary to bag the fish on high-humidity nights.

People have asked me how safe the Cold Method is because of the amount of time the fish are hanging out in the open. Tests have shown that the bacteria count is actually highest in fish dried indoors under controlled conditions.

Steps 1-3: Gut, Split, and Pierce.
The same as steps 1-3 under *The Smoke Method*. In less than ideal conditions, skin the fish to reduce drying time.

Step 4: Choose a Site.
Requirements:
- **A Constant Breeze.** Hillsides, valleys, and beaches are likely places.
- **Low Humidity.** The higher off the ground, the dryer the air.
- **Protection from Elements and Scavengers.** Consider protected tree branches or an elevated, roofed structure.

Step 5: Suspend Splits under Canopy.

Mount them securely so that they can withstand winds, and allow enough space between them for ample air circulation.

Step 6: Check Periodically for Decay.

A sulfur or ammonia odor means rot. Salvage by trimming, and address the cause of the rot.

Step 7: Drive out Remaining Moisture.

When several of the thickest splits, that have been warmed to around 70°F, prove to be dry to the touch all the way through, crisp them in a frying pan or on a hot rock to drive out any remaining moisture. **If dried fish is all you need**, stop processing at this point, pack in airtight containers, and skip to step 11.

To prevent moisture reabsorption, continue through the next steps without interruption.

Step 8: Debone.

To expose the bones, bend the splits by folding the skin upon itself.

Step 9: Flake.

Crumble the flesh with your fingers to work it off of the skin.

Step 10: Blend and Pack.

Add oil/lard in a one-to-two ratio with the fish, mix thoroughly, and pack tightly into airtight pint-to-quart size containers. Be sure to squeeze out all air.

Step 11: Store.

The same as under *The Smoke Method*.

The Hot Method

When time is of the essence, and when you have lean fish, this is the method to use. It is also a good fallback when conditions are not suitable for the Cold Method. The drying process can be finished in one day, even with large fish, by splitting the splits to thin them.

The ideal temperature for this method is 50 to 60°F, which gives the best drying conditions and temperature differential to create the strong updraft that powers this method. Like the Smoke Method, this one can be made to work in a variety of weather conditions.

Steps 1-3: Gut, Split, and Pierce.

The same as steps 1-3 under *The Smoke Method*, except that tail-connected splits cannot be used, as both flesh sides must face the fire. To speed up drying time for big fish, halve the splits.

Step 4: Build a Radiant Fire.

With hardwood, create a hot, concentrated, bed of coals with low flame. We want to create a strong updraft to facilitate drying, so choose a protected site where the breeze will not interfere.

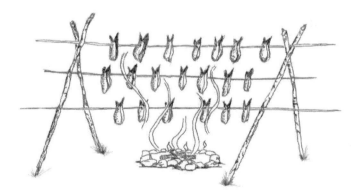

Step 5: Hang Splits on A-Frame.

Construct a stick A-frame to set over the fire, and hang the splits on the frame, with the flesh side facing to the coals.

Step 6: Monitor.

Carefully regulate the size of the fire and the distance of the splits from it, to maximize the updraft and keep the splits warm but not cooking.

Steps 7-10: Debone, Flake, Blend, Pack, and Store.

The same steps as under the Cold Method. To prevent moisture reabsorption, continue through these steps without interruption. If the process takes more than one day, bag and hang the fish for the night, so that they do not reabsorb moisture or get scavenged.

And now for dessert. With a carcass that is too far gone to salvage, maggots may be the only edible part. And with a fresher carcass, they could provide a garnish that is every bit as nourishing as some of the prime cuts. The juicy little guys don't taste so bad either. For how to safely prepare and eat them, follow the instructions in my upcoming book on survival foraging. Refer back to the Introduction for more information.

Acknowledgments

I first wish to honor my teachers: the Native Elders and the pack of Wolves I lived with. They deserve the bulk of the credit for this book, as I'd no doubt still be bumbling around if they hadn't passed their skills and wisdom on to me.

Yet knowledge alone doesn't make a book any more than a pile of lumber makes a house. It takes craftsmanship, and for that I extend my deepest gratitude to editors Leslie Stager and Melissa Kay Bishop. Leslie was somehow able to take my rough notes and shape them into a respectable first draft, which Melissa fleshed out and backed with research. However, her talents don't stop there, as she also rendered the illustrations and initial layout.

Recognition for this book's attractive and well-crafted finishing touches go to Julie Plumitis for the front and back covers, and to her and Michael Fox for the inner layout.

There is hardly ever a reason for someone to starve—in any circumstance—and I commend my clients and students over the years for showing what people of any background or skill level are capable of when the going gets tough.

About the Author

A specialist in the old Indian survival skills, Tamarack Song serves as a consultant for wilderness trekkers around the world, and for organizations such as the National Geographic Society. He founded the Teaching Drum Outdoor School, where he offers survival and nature-immersion courses that train people to survive entirely by their own wits. For forty years he has provided all of his family's protein needs from the wilds, without relying on weapons, steel traps, or fishing tackle. He has picked up roadkill and scavenged the kills of other animals for that long as well. To learn more about Tamarack and his writings, visit www.tamaracksong.org.

About Teaching Drum Outdoor School

Founded in 1987 by the author, the Teaching Drum offers instruction in the full range of wilderness and emergency survival skills. They are taught the way Tamarack learned them years ago from the Woodland Indians.

Teaching Drum Outdoor School is truly an *outdoor* school. The classroom is the wilderness, where all courses are held. It is a survival school in the ultimate sense, as students learn how to not only stay alive, but thrive, even if they are caught without gear or equipment.

Skills must be learned well enough to rely on in extreme situations. In the advanced courses, students eat their food raw if they cannot start a friction fire without tools, from whatever wood they find laying around.

Learn more about the Teaching Drum—the only school of its kind—at www.teachingdrum.org.

Printed in Great Britain
by Amazon